Donor Conception Network

Our Family:
A guide for the relatives and friends
of those contemplating donor conception,
undergoing treatment or parenting young
donor conceived children

By
Olivia Montuschi

Olivia Montuschi

Olivia Montuschi is the mother of two donor conceived young people, born in 1983 and 1986. She and her husband Walter Merricks founded the Donor Conception Network with four other families in 1993. Olivia trained as a teacher and a counsellor and for many years worked as a parenting educator and trainer, writing materials and running parenting education programmes. She now works part-time as Practice Consultant to DC Network.

Donor Conception Network

ISBN 978-1-910222-26-3

Published by the
Donor Conception Network,
154 Caledonian Road, London N1 9RD

Telephone: 020 7278 2608
email: enquiries@dcnetwork.org
www.dcnetwork.org

Contents

Methodology

This booklet, and the companion volume for parents of donor conceived children entitled Telling and Talking with Family and Friends about Donor Conception, was a long time in the making. It was August 2009 when the idea of writing something to help parents and would-be parents share information about donor conception with friends and family was first mooted in the Donor Conception Network's (DC Network or DCN) eBulletin. The response from members and mental health professionals from all over the world was enthusiastic. Everyone was beginning to notice that telling relatives and friends about the use of donor conception in family building was now felt by many people to be more difficult than sharing information with donor conceived children.

DC Network celebrated its twentieth birthday in 2013. As one of the founders I feel privileged to have spoken with many thousands of families over these years. This, plus my own experience of being part of a donor conception family for 30 years informs my general approach to this booklet. In addition, in special preparation for writing about this particular topic, I researched the literature currently available about sharing information on general infertility, bereavement, cancer, mental illness etc. with family and friends. The research literature on the sharing of information about donor conception is small and well known to me. It has, however, been enriched by the Relative Strangers project conducted between 1st October 2010 and 30th June 2013 by the Morgan Centre at Manchester University and these booklets have benefitted from the findings. DC Network also ran a national conference on Talking with Family and Friends and at this I organised an exercise to help members think around the subject. This resulted in over 100 written responses and many email addresses inviting me to follow up with a personal interview.

Acknowledgements and thanks

Enormous thanks go first of all to the Nuffield Foundation without whose funding support this booklet would have remained a wish rather than a reality.

I am indebted to DC Network members Jane Ellis, Ruth Yudkin, Caroline Spencer, Marion Scott and Natasha Canfer for their very constructive comments on and additions to the text as it emerged. Both the content and the way it is expressed improved immeasurably as a result. Thanks also to Marion for additional mentoring services. Final thanks to my beloved husband Walter who writes so beautifully himself and whose fluent command of the English language drives me to despair and admiration in equal parts.

The people without whom this booklet would not have been possible are those DC Network members who took part in the Fears and Successes exercise at the national conference in September 2012, and particularly those of you I met or spoke to on the 'phone over the following months. Also to those members who responded to my request in DCN's eBulletin for people willing to talk with me on this topic. Thank you all very much for being so generous with your time and stories. By contributing to this booklet you are almost certainly helping many, many others feel more comfortable and confident about talking with family and friends.

Our Family

"We live in a small rural community so I was worried about others knowing, but people I have told have been very understanding and had a lot of respect for us."

Annabel, mother to sperm donor conceived one-year-old

Introduction

Welcome to this short booklet which is intended for the close family and friends of a couple or single woman for whom donor conception is either a potential or already an actual method of creating or adding to a family. They may be using, or already have used, sperm, egg, double (egg and sperm) or embryo donation for this purpose. It is most likely that you will be reading this at a time when they are still contemplating donor conception, going through treatment, pregnant or parenting a young child and this is the assumption made throughout. The reason they have given you this booklet to read is that they want you to understand more about this way of forming a family and what it may mean for them and for you.

As a reader of this booklet you may be a parent, grandparent, sibling, aunt, uncle, cousin or other relative – or a close friend – of the people concerned. The term 'relative or friend' will be used throughout to cover these different relationships.

The news about donor conception may or may not have come as a shock or a surprise to you. You may be wondering how to respond but not know the best way to go about it or you may feel very comfortable with the idea from the start. If it all feels very new to you it may take a while to get used to the idea and you may find that your feelings change during this process.

Having a child by donor conception is a 'different' way for a child to come into a family. These days parents are encouraged to tell their children about donor conception from an early age and most manage this, although sometimes with some trepidation. However, the anticipation of talking with family and friends remains fraught for many. DC Network members often mention a fear of being judged or rejected because of the choices they have made.

Warm and supportive relationships with close relatives and friends are enormously important to potential and actual parents of donor conceived children, as they are for all families. By just 'being there' for the parents you can help them feel confident and comfortable enough to provide the nurturing, stable and open environment in which their children can thrive and be proud of their beginnings.

Your relative or friend is likely to have been, or still is, going through a huge amount emotionally. They will also have become very knowledgeable about donor conception, the treatments, the technicalities, the law and the implications of creating a family this way. Many will have been on a very long journey to reach this point, involving much heartache on the way. Some others, where infertility has been known about for many years or where a man has had a vasectomy rather than being primarily infertile, may be less shocked but nevertheless needing your support around using donor conception.

Because you are an important person in their life your relative or friend would like you to know what is or has been happening in their life so that you can support them in the best way possible.

In the following pages you will find some clues as to what your relatives or friends have been going through. If you are a parent or sibling you could be feeling some sense of loss or confusion about what is going on in your family and this is acknowledged too. Also set out will be the reasons why openness with children and others is now considered to be best for the whole family. At the end of the booklet you will find a blue shaded section about Infertility and Donor Conception: the facts, the practicalities and the law. You may want to turn to this first or ignore it completely, concentrating on the social and emotional impact of donor conception for your relative or friend and you.

Most people having fertility treatment in the UK conceive with the help of a donor who is anonymous at the time of treatment, but will be identifiable to children from age 18, so the main focus of the booklet is on this situation. The majority of the booklet is also appropriate for those who have conceived abroad using an anonymous donor. In addition you will find a section on some of the different issues for those using a donor who is known to them. Many of the chapters are appropriate for those who are close to couples or individuals using any type of donor (see highlighted section at the end of the booklet for description of the differences).

At the back you will find some bullet points about helpful things to say and do.

How your relatives or friends are feeling

It is very rare for people to set out on their family building journey planning to use donated eggs, sperm or embryos. Those seeking to avoid a heritable disorder are the exception, as are single women and lesbian and gay couples.

People have often been through extensive invasive tests and many cycles of unsuccessful treatment over several years before reaching the point of considering gamete donation. The journey to having a child can be very long and when egg, sperm or embryo donation becomes the only way to make this possible, then time needs to be set aside to grieve the child that could not be, before going on to hopefully have the one that is possible... sometimes referred to by parents as the one they were meant to have.

The pain of unwanted childlessness is visceral but because the loss (of the child they cannot conceive) is invisible to outsiders it is often difficult to understand for those who have conceived easily or do not feel the need to have children.

Anyone trying to conceive tends to live from month to month, cycle to cycle, with emotional turmoil resulting from each negative pregnancy test or period starting. It is exhausting and can feel soul destroying. It is also a very challenging time. Men and women often approach and handle fertility issues very differently. Lesbian couples, only one of whom may be going through treatment, may have differences too. All partners need to have tolerance and respect for the way their other half is managing the feelings and the process, but this can be difficult when emotions run high, as they often do. Single women are managing alone a process that is going to be life changing and as such value supportive networks of family and friends enormously, although they too sometimes need solitude. How much they wish to share with others may change from month to month and week to week.

Parents and others can be a wonderful source of support, but because of the toll that fertility treatment can take on a couple or an individual they occasionally need to withdraw from others, even close family members, for a while. This can cause hurt when it is misunderstood. Sometimes even well-meaning words of reassurance or encouragement can cause upset at a vulnerable time. The emotional and practical impact of on-going fertility issues and treatments is enormous and some women and men prefer to talk with professionals or others in a similar situation for a while. On-line forums are often used for peer support with great effect.

It is now widely recognised that loss of fertility, of the ability to contribute to the creation of a child with a loved partner, is a grief that needs to be negotiated with the aid of time, nurture and support from those we love. Both partners equally need this care, whether or not they are the one with the fertility problem. Men hurt as well as women, although some may disguise their pain behind bravado. Men's grief, particularly when the reason for donor conception is male factor infertility, is often underestimated. It can be assumed that the wish for a child is greater for women than men, but although a woman may grieve not being able to have the child of the man she loves, there is always the consolation of being able to go through pregnancy and hopefully breastfeed, like any other woman. Infertile men have to manage their sense of perceived inadequacy at not being able to contribute to the making of a baby without the comfort of being able to nurture their baby in the womb.

> "I turned to the counsellor and I said, 'Well, how do you deal with this stuff?' She said 'The truth is, you don't, you kind of live with it.' Which was a nice sort of thing and I think it helped me massively, that speech. It means you don't have to come out the other side and everything be OK, you just live with it and you deal with it and you try and let it affect you as little as possible."
> Trevor, quoted in Key Messages from the Relative Strangers research.

Single women, with fertility difficulties or not, may grieve for the loss of the partner they had always assumed they would be making a family with and for the loss of life as a two-parent family. If they find that donor eggs are needed as well as donor sperm, then there is grieving – like any woman – for her lost fertility and loss of a genetic connection to any child she has.

Going through a period of sadness seems to be an important component of a process that allows everyone, as couples and individually, to adjust to the reality of their situation before making good decisions about the way forward. The timescale is different for everyone. Single women also often spend time carefully considering whether they have the emotional and financial resources to go it alone. For some people, though not everyone, donor conception will become the right way for them to become parents. In fact most parents cannot imagine having different children and wouldn't swap genetically connected ones for the family they have: a second choice, but not second best.

The role of family and friends

Your understanding of their state of mind is what your relative or friend needs. Before they have conceived, they may go through times when they find it hard to attend family or other social occasions where there are pregnant women, babies or small children. Christmas (or other religious festivals), weddings, baby showers and christenings tend to be the hardest to face. They are not being difficult, they are in pain and need your quiet acceptance and support. A squeeze of the hand to show you understand is often enough.

If your relative or friend is at the treatment stage of donor conception, do wait for them to tell you how it is going and try to avoid asking. Particularly if they have had previous unsuccessful cycles they may not announce a pregnancy until the 12 or 14 week stage. In the meantime you may be aware of heightened mood or that the woman is avoiding all the foods and substances it is suggested pregnant women should not have. Keep quiet, have patience. Good news will definitely be given in time and celebrations can then take place. Unsuccessful cycles may or may not be communicated, but you may be aware of lowered mood or social withdrawal as a result. You may feel that a simple, 'I'm so sorry' is the best first response if you are told.

Parents and siblings

As a sibling or parent of anyone undertaking donor conception you will have your own thoughts and feelings about this which may well include sadness and grief. These feelings are likely to be partly about what your relative is having to deal with but also possibly about the lost genetic connection or complicated feelings you don't necessarily understand yourself about donor conception. You may feel guilty about these and your own sense of loss but they are very normal feelings you are absolutely entitled to. What is important is that you acknowledge them to yourself, talk with your partner or others, but preferably not the person concerned, and seek support and help from a professional if necessary.

Recent research has found that parents of those needing donor conception often bear a huge burden of care and support for them and struggle to find appropriate support for themselves, particularly if they are sworn to secrecy. DC Network is committed to offering support to all family members and welcomes grandparents or others getting in touch.

Men and women in all family types who find they need the help of a donor often feel very guilty about having, as they see it, let their parents down. If infertile, they can feel a failure for not being able to fulfil the reproductive functions of a man or woman and a double failure for not being able to give their parents genetically connected grandchildren. Letting them know that they are loved and valued for themselves, without necessarily talking directly about donor conception issues, can be helpful.

Friends

It is a mark of the closeness of the friendship they feel that your friend has decided to share this private information with you. She or he will have thought long and hard about who they can trust to be supportive and understanding. They are unlikely to have told everyone.

Close friends are enormously important to all potential and actual parents but particularly to single women who can worry about how having a baby on their own will affect their friendships. If your friend is a single women contemplating becoming a solo mum, you can be of enormous support to her by just being there and offering reassurance that she is resourceful while she goes through her own decision-making process.

If she is still at the deciding stage, don't be surprised if her thoughts and emotions vary, but usually once a decision is really taken, most single women become quite determined about this journey to motherhood. They hope their friends will support them even if it is not what they would do themselves.

Painful decisions

If you find for whatever reason that you cannot immediately be positive or even neutral about donor conception, please try to respect the decisions that your relative or friend has made and keep your feelings to yourself. People long for their parents, in particular, to support them, but as adults they have to make their own decisions about their lives. If they are regularly on the receiving end of negative or hostile remarks or behaviour they may decide, very reluctantly, that not seeing you very often – or ever – is the only thing they can do. This would be a very sad loss for all concerned.

Donor conception can challenge how we think about families

Sperm, egg or embryo donation is not a cure for infertility but it allows infertile heterosexual couples, single women and lesbian and gay couples to build families. All will have a strong intention to parent, and parent well, and will have given considerable thought to what it means to create a family using gametes from another person. They may have started off feeling that a genetic connection to their child is an absolute requirement for parenthood and it may be that you feel this way also. However, during the grieving period many people slowly revise their views, discovering that loving relationships, commitment and shared values are the foundation of a family. They move from despair to hope as they realise that donor conception gives them the opportunity to go through pregnancy and birth, building a family that has a 'difference' but has been created through love in the same way as any other.

If you tend towards feeling that genetic connections are the only real basis for including someone in 'the family', I invite you to reconsider. The modern family is rarely mum and dad and genetically connected 2.4 children. Many children live apart from one parent or in re-formed families where there are children from each partner's previous relationship. Children are raised by grandparents, by single mums and dads and by same sex partnerships. All can do well if there is a strong intention and commitment to parenting and the family is well supported. Donor conception families, particularly heterosexual couples, are amongst the least complex of modern families. Research has shown that ALL types of donor conception families do at least as well as or better in terms of family warmth and functioning than those where children were conceived without donor help.

Older generations are sometimes, but not inevitably, more inclined towards keeping 'difference' under wraps. Feelings used not to be talked about so freely and infertility was considered something to be kept private, if not actually shameful in itself. Single parenthood by choice and same sex couple parenting are fairly recent phenomena that would have been impossible or concealed because of significant stigma only a short time ago. Thirty years ago when my husband and I discovered that sperm donation was the only way we were going to be able to have a family, clinics suggested that no-one was told about donor conception. You may have assumed that any child conceived this way would not be told how they came into the family.

If you find yourself feeling embarrassed by what you are being told and wonder why this topic needs to be talked about at all, you may want to say something like, 'I'm finding this a bit difficult. How about writing it all down for me so I can take it in in my own time." Although some parents insist that their child's grandparents acknowledge the fact of donor conception, many others respect their own parents' reticence on the topic, particularly if grandparents are warm, loving and accepting of the child. If you have a good relationship with your son or daughter who is using donor conception it should hopefully be possible to ask them to respect your wish not to have conversations that make you feel uncomfortable. In turn you could show your support with gestures like an arm round the shoulders or a squeeze of the hand. When it comes to a young child mentioning their conception to you, however, you may have to prepare yourself with some simple responses like, 'I know, mummy told me'. The chapter on Openness below will hopefully give some insights into why talking about infertility and donor conception are considered to be better for the whole family these days.

> "My parents completely accepted that their grandson had been conceived by egg donation but assumed that we wouldn't be telling him. However, they 'got it' straight away when we explained that we were going to be open from the start."
> Catherine, mum to egg-donation conceived son

Openness

Over the last 20 years there has been a sea change in attitudes to sharing information with children and significant others about donor conception. In 2005 clinical psychologist Diane Ehrensaft noted,

"...the social tides have changed. As they have changed, experts have done a 180 degree turn in their thinking about disclosure. Twenty years ago people thought disclosure would be traumatic for the child, humiliating to the parent and disrupt the parent-child bond. Now it is believed to be a violation of the child's rights, a denial of reality and a threat to the integrity of the family not to tell a child the truth about his or her birth history."

'Telling' and 'openness' are now recognised as important for children not just by counsellors and psychologists but also by bodies such as the Human Fertilisation and Embryology Authority (HFEA), the Human Genetics Commission, the UK Government and the American Society of Reproductive Medicine. All UK fertility clinics have to provide information about openness being best for children and families and guidance as to where materials for sharing information with children can be obtained.

The Donor Conception Network was founded on the principle that openness with children puts in place a solid underpinning of honesty and trust within a family, these qualities being the foundations on which healthy relationships are built. It is respectful of each individual child/young person and the adult they will become that they are not deceived about the genetic links within the family. This could potentially lead to mis-diagnosis of medical conditions and life decisions being based on false information.

Research has shown that children who did not find out about their donor conception until they were teenagers or adults often felt there was something wrong in their family, knew it was to do with them but did not know what it was. Some thought they had been adopted and others were sure their mother had had an affair. Such a situation led in some cases to poor self-esteem and undermined trust in the family. Secrets can also be very hard to keep, particularly when family talk turns to likenesses and parents find themselves being evasive and sometimes directly lying. The difficult feelings generated by such deceptions are those that lead children to suspect there is something wrong.

These days the advice is to start the telling process early, preferably from infancy and definitely before the age of five. In this way the story is built up over several years and the child does not remember a time when they did not know. It is also helpful for parents to practise the language of telling the story early so that they become comfortable with it. Parents sometimes feel very anxious about starting to 'tell' as they fear a change in the relationship with their much-loved child. However, love, consistency and an emotional environment based on trust are much more important to young children than genetics and rejection is the last thing on children's minds. DC Network publishes picture/story books entitled *Our Story* that can be used to help begin to tell children in simple, age appropriate language and *Telling and*

Talking booklets for parents to help them find the right timing and language for telling. You may find these books of interest too.

Parents are encouraged to share the information about how their family came into being with close relatives and friends who will continue to be part of their life. This is so that you can be ready if and when the child concerned mentions, "the nice lady who gave an egg to help mummy have me". Other people who should have the information are the child's GP and teachers, who can then knowledgeably support a child if they choose to talk about donor conception at school. But of course not everyone needs to know. Acquaintances and strangers who comment on a child's likeness to a parent or even grandparent – and it is extraordinary how often this happens – can easily be answered with a smile or generalisation. Privacy is what every family deserves. It is secrecy that can be harmful.

The information that is being shared with you is privileged. How a child has been conceived is rarely public knowledge when help has not been needed and parents have a right to consider the information private, until and unless they choose to tell others. Just occasionally the information could lead to a child being picked on or discriminated against, particularly if they live in a community where 'difference' could be a source of bullying. It is always right to ask your relative or friend if you may share donor conception information with others, both inside and outside the family. It may be relevant to also ask who else knows, but remember that the last thing your relative or friend will want is to feel that everyone is having a good old gossip at their expense. Make it clear that that's not your motivation or intention.

If you are at a large social gathering it is important to remember that not everyone in the room may have the same level of information as you.

> Jennie was shocked when her brother introduced her as mother to an egg donation child at a social event where there were both people who knew and didn't know about donor conception. She wished she had been clearer with him from the start about how far the privileged information he had could be shared.

Talking with your relative or friend

You may or may not feel comfortable with the topic of donor conception or infertility. You may feel you don't know what to say or would actually prefer to avoid the subject, but as mentioned above, some acknowledgement from you that you appreciate what they are going through, or have been through, is likely to be helpful to them. It doesn't have to be a long conversation. And again, a kind look or a squeeze of the hand can be very meaningful.

If you feel you would like some support in managing your own feelings about donor conception and don't feel you can talk with your relative or friend about it, DC Network can help, either directly or with a list of trusted counsellors.

If you are able to 'be there' for your relative or friend then the most important thing you can do is listen...to the words they say and the feelings behind the words. Ask them what it is they need from you and recognise that their needs will change from day to day as they move through the process...of deciding, treatment and then hopefully pregnancy and raising a child.

The opposite to those who would prefer to avoid the topic, are those who find donor conception fascinating and want to ask all sorts of questions about the donor, the medical procedures and even how much it all costs. Whilst some couples or individuals may be happy to provide such details, many find these sorts of questions intrusive. It's almost as if sharing something as intimate as information about donor conception and/or infertility is perceived as having removed the boundaries that would normally be observed in a friendship or family relationship. If you find yourself wanting to ask a lot of questions it may be helpful to take a step back first and ask yourself how knowing the answer is going to contribute to supporting your friend or relative. If it isn't then you might want to curb your curiosity or check if it is OK to ask questions.

Donor conception issues do not end with the birth of a child, so it is not helpful to say that everything will be the same once the baby is born. Of course all families with a new baby are completely preoccupied with the practical and emotional demands of parenting. Donor conception themes definitely fade into the background. However, recognition of some on-going issues is supportive of the tasks and responsibilities that parents by donor conception need to manage.

Talking with cousins or children of friends

Several of the parents I talked to as part of my research for both booklets were anxious about whether, when or how their nephews and nieces – cousins of their children – should learn about the donor conception of their own children. If you are a sibling or close friend of someone with a donor conceived child and are a parent yourself, you may have wondered about whether and how you should talk with your own children.

Parents often fear that once a cousin realises that their uncle or aunt's child does not share a genetic connection, thoughtless or hurtful remarks may be made. Although this is unlikely to happen unless there are other rivalries or jealousy involved, young children make their own interpretations of what we say and can be very direct.

"Mummy says your Daddy isn't your real Daddy."

When thinking about what your own children need to know, the lead should always come from the donor conceived child's parents. Talk with them about the level of information they are happy to have shared and the language they would like you to use. But the principle is the same as for other people in the donor conceived child's inner circle. If your child spends a lot of time with your sibling's or friend's child, sharing family events, meals and perhaps holidays, then they should have some basic understanding about donor conception that can be built upon, without emphasis or fuss, as they grow and ask questions.

When talking with any child the most important factor to take into account is their stage of development, which may not be the same as their age in years. The building blocks of information sharing are exactly the same as talking with donor conceived children themselves. The *Telling and Talking* booklets, which are organised around children's developmental stages, could be of help here and you may want to get hold of the one that is appropriate for your child's age.

If cousins or friends are under five or six then it can be helpful for you to talk with them in a very general way about the different ways that families are made and that sometimes mummies and daddies, mummies alone or two mummies need help from someone else to make a baby. Letting them know that a sperm and egg (or special cells) from a man and a woman are needed to make a baby is important too. You may want to use some of the language from the *Our Story* books for donor conceived children, like 'kind man or woman' to refer to the donor. When you have done this for a while, you can then say something along the lines of, "And that's how your cousin Sammy was made. Aunty Jo needed an egg from another woman to help make him."

If your children are seven, eight or older when the donor conceived child comes on the scene, then a more direct approach may be required, although some talk about sameness and differences in other families they know can be helpful as well. At any age, using a 'hook' provided by a child, as in their asking about how babies are made, or as a result of a TV programme about children/families, can be a very natural way in to talking about donor conception.

Language

The language of donor conception can be a tricky area to negotiate. Whilst a genetic connection to the donor should always be acknowledged, a genetic link alone does not confer parenthood. This is established through intention and commitment to parenting, as well as by legal means. It is, therefore, never helpful to refer to the donor as the 'real' mother or father, even if she or he is a known person.

Sometimes when talking about 'likenesses' in a family (and this comes up a lot in conversations around children) relatives or friends can innocently say, "If he were yours then his hair would probably be curlier"...or something along those lines. The word 'yours' can plunge a dagger into the heart of a non-genetic mother or father or their partner. They are very clear that this child is his or hers because they are raising them and could not love them more, but feel this fact is being denied, albeit inadvertently, by the speaker.

Good rules to follow are: listen to the language that is used by the parent(s), don't be afraid to ask about appropriate terminology and think before you speak.

See sections at the end for lists of dos and don'ts.

When faith or culture is an issue

You may be finding that your own faith or culture is an issue when it comes to accepting or supporting your relative or friend in relation to donor conception.

If your faith is shared with them, put yourself in their shoes and try to imagine their struggle with their beliefs and principles. Their whole being longs to be a parent, but your shared God appears to be forbidding them from going through procedures that would enable their dream to come true.

Karen said that for her it was a six-year spiritual journey to feeling comfortable about making the decision that sperm donation was an acceptable way of having a child. She had had to negotiate a space between herself and her God where it was possible to come to this conclusion.

"In order for my desire for a child to be OK, I had to think about what it means to create life and also what being donor conceived would mean for a child."

Donor conception is never undertaken lightly. Those raised in a strong faith tradition that disapproves of third-party conception face enormously difficult decisions that will test them to their limits. All faiths support the bringing of children into the world. It may be that you will have to respect a decision by the couple or individual concerned that allows them to come to a personal interpretation of this teaching.

If your relative or friend does not share your faith or culture then maybe you could consider putting aside your own views and simply empathise with their wish to become parents. Telling them that you love or care about them and that you know they will make decisions that are right for them, can be very supportive whilst not compromising your own beliefs.

The American Fertility Association produces some excellent leaflets on issues to do with infertility and third party conception for all family types. The following is a quote from *"Keeping Your Faith: How a Religious Framework Helps (or Hurts) You"* by Marie Davidson Ph.D.

"As human beings we are connected to all our communities, our families, our social networks, our work colleagues and our faith communities. They are all capable of helping or hurting us as we try to build a family. The hurt comes from the judgement and lack of understanding. The help comes from the support and loving connections. People who struggle with infertility always say that the second worst pain of all (after being infertile in the first place) is from what other people say/do or not say/ not do. What is a sharper knife thrust than these remarks? 'It's God's will.' 'It's not natural (to do that treatment).' 'God has other plans for you'. 'Maybe you weren't meant to be a mother/father.' So who amongst us has a direct line to God's plan for anyone? When a patient asks, "Why is God doing this to me? I think I am a good person." I think about how many truly wonderful people I get to meet in my work who are struggling to be parents. And I say, 'I do have a God concept (ever-evolving) and I think that if 'my' God is deciding who gets to be a parent, then S/He has a really lousy track record.' This has an effect. People smile, even chuckle, and usually see how irrational it seems to think God controls this being a parent thing. I hope you will too."

When the donor is known

A known donor rather than an identifiable donor, is someone who is personally known to the potential recipient of donated eggs or sperm. It may be a family member, close friend, someone from an acquaintance group or a person who has advertised their services as a donor on the internet. Egg, sperm or embryo donation treatments that take place in a UK licensed clinic give legal protections to all parties to donation. Everyone involved in a known donation via a UK clinic also has an opportunity to have at least one counselling session per person to make sure that they understand the short and long-term implications of donation. This will include the role that the donor is expected to take (if any) in the child's life, how he or she will be known and referred to and the kind of contact that is expected by all.

Sperm donation that takes place privately may be the result of a number of different decisions, arrangements and expectations. A single woman or a lesbian couple, and occasionally heterosexual couples, may enter into an arrangement whereby the donor agrees to be available to the child either from birth or at some point in the future. There may or may not be frequent contact between donor and child. Alternatively there may be a co-parenting arrangement with a man who is part donor and part father to a child.

Recent research has found that non-birth mothers in lesbian families sometimes fear that a known donor might be treated as the 'real' second parent of the child, thus pushing them to the margins. Some couples overcome this by either using anonymous donation or by arranging donation through a clinic and thus securing the legal parenthood of the non-genetic mother.

> Claudia: My real concern was I would feel that Nina and the donor had a baby together and I was a spare.
> *Key Messages from the Relative Strangers research*

In all known donor situations where treatment takes place outside of a licensed clinic all parties should have supportive counselling and sign a written agreement drawn up in consultation with a solicitor before going ahead with inseminations. Unfortunately a number of known donor arrangements break down because not enough time and attention has been paid beforehand to crystallising everyone's expectations. The actual birth of a child can trigger unexpected nurturing feelings in a donor or cause a parent to feel more protective of their privacy than they had anticipated.

If your relative or friend is contemplating known donation or has a child conceived by a known donor, then guidance from them will be helpful in knowing how to refer to the donor, particularly when talking with the child.

Particular issues for lesbian mothers and single women

Single women and lesbian couples, all face the question of explaining to others what is going on when a pregnancy becomes obvious, if they have not done so before. For both lesbian and solo mum families it is often the family type, rather than the issue of donor conception, that is more dominant once a child is born.

Lesbians

It is much more common these days for lesbian couples to have children, although having them as a couple, rather than raising children from previous heterosexual relationships, remains a newish family form. It is possible that although you knew about your daughter's or sibling's sexuality before, it has been brought into sharper focus through pregnancy or birth of a child. Some parents of lesbians find that becoming a grandparent can be a way to mend previously difficult relationships through mutual love and affection for the new baby.

> Priscilla: My mum was okay. She doesn't like the fact that I'm a lesbian but I think I've redeemed myself by….
> Meredith (partner): Being a fifties housewife. (laughter)
> *From Key Messages from the Relative Strangers research.*

Donor conception is usually a wholly positive choice for lesbian couples, untinged by the disappointments and feelings of failure so often experienced by heterosexual couples and single women. There can, however, be some sadness if one partner is infertile or too old to be the birth mother, and it is wise not to assume a straightforward journey to conception.

Lesbians have no choice about sharing information about being donor conceived with their children and usually start to do so from an early age. Children in lesbian couple and solo mum families often start to ask about 'having a dad' from as early as age two, and if these questions are likely to come your way too, it is important that you ask about what sort of answers to give.

Whilst the birth mother's position is, for the most part, identical to that of her heterosexual peers, the role of the non-birth mother is not so clear-cut. It is, therefore, particularly important for family, friends, teachers and others to be sensitive to this and confirm her status as an equal mother. It is also helpful if the parental name (eg other mummy/mummy Jane or whatever the non-birth mother is known by) can be sensitively noted by others and used when talking with the child or others. Listening carefully to how the couple use language gives the very best guide for you to follow as a supportive relative or friend.

For lesbians in a partnership which is perhaps not known about by everyone, pregnancy can mean having to 'come out' to work colleagues, health professionals or even just people they meet at the ante-natal clinic or in the supermarket...and certainly once a child is born to child minders, nursery schools etc. In fact for a lesbian mother, mentioning having children in any situation means coming out as a lesbian family time and time again, the presumption of heterosexuality in relation to children remaining so strong generally. This can be wearing, even if the response is positive or neutral.

People are sometimes very curious about how lesbian families work and some DC Network members have spoken about being subjected to intrusive – although rarely hostile – questioning about family roles. Whilst most lesbian couples are happy to have their particular family form acknowledged, like any other family they deserve privacy with regard to their private lives. There is a fine line to be struck between being attuned to 'getting it right' for them and treating this particular sort of family just like anyone else. This is best achieved through being attentive, listening to the language the family use and following their lead.

Single women – solo mums

Most single heterosexual women using donor conception for family creation would much prefer to have had a child within a conventional relationship. Many, finding themselves single towards the end of their thirties or early forties take the courageous decision to have a child before their fertility declines further, whilst not giving up on the idea of finding a partner at some future time. There is often as much loss and the need for grieving involved in this decision as there is for couples when infertility is the reason for donor conception. That said, there is also a huge amount of excitement and hope invested in donor conception as a way to create a family...one that will be formed as much through love as any other.

The vast majority of single women think enormously hard about the emotional, practical and financial aspects of becoming a solo mum before taking any action at all. If they suspect that relatives and friends who are important to them might not approve then they are likely to have thought even harder about the decision before going ahead.

Friendship is hugely important to single women who are often older, may live far from family or have parents who are very elderly or have died. They worry about how friends will react, how having a child may change the relationship, as well as how they will juggle being a good friend with mothering and working to support this new family.

Announcing a pregnancy when a woman is single and perhaps presumed by everyone to be focused on her career and not interested in babies, can feel fraught in anticipation. The reality for many, however, is that work colleagues offer congratulations and are very accepting once they know the woman herself is pleased about being pregnant. The focus tends to be more on the practicalities of how long she will work for, maternity leave etc.

Charlotte said that her own expectations of having a family in a more conventional situation, affected how she felt about sharing information with others about her pregnancy, which she sometimes jokingly refers to as her 'immaculate conception.' She said that the most helpful thing people could say was, "If you are happy about this, then I'm delighted for you" and probe no further. Although her mother would have preferred her to adopt, she has put aside her own feelings to completely support Charlotte.

Interviewed shortly before she was to give birth, Charlotte was aware that being on her own with her baby will trigger further questions about 'the father' and she is expecting to have to remain alert to situations where questions might arise.

Single women who have conceived by an anonymous but identifiable donor in a clinic are likely to use the word 'donor' with their child. Those who have used a known donor may use that person's first name or even the terms 'father or dad' depending on the agreement that has been made with the donor. It is always right to check before using any particular terminology. As they grow up you will need to check intermittently what the child knows about his or her conception and how your friend talks to them.

Ultimately single women want to be accepted for who they are and the decisions they have taken. They very much hope that the people who are important to them will offer support during this exciting transition and be ready to welcome their long awaited baby with love. Offers of practical help are usually very welcome too!

Final thoughts

It is of course not only single women but everyone using donor conception who hope that you, their closest relatives and friends, will open your hearts to their children. No baby could be more wanted than one conceived with help from a donor.

I hope this booklet has given you the information and the tools you need to understand both the practicalities and the emotional rollercoaster ridden by men and women who find that donor conception is their best route to having the family they long for. No-one will have thought longer or harder about what they are doing.

In addition you may want to have a look at DC Network's website, www.dcnetwork.org. Of particular interest may be the *Letter Leaflets* from experienced parents to those just starting out and the four *Telling and Talking* booklets. Your relative or friend is likely to be delighted if you do.

Dos and don'ts

Do

- Ask what it is they need from you.

- Listen carefully...to the words and the feelings behind them.

- Ask about the terminology and language they would like you to use.

- Try to put yourself in their shoes and think about the language you use and comments you make.

- Indicate that you are happy to listen or talk when they are ready but that you understand if this is not what they want

- Be particularly sensitive about announcing your own or someone else's pregnancy.

- Think carefully about invitations to events where babies and young children may be present, but do not make your relative or friend feel excluded.

- Respect the decisions made by your relative or friend.

- Help support the decisions made, even if they are not ones you would have made yourself.

- Understand that during the treatment stage withdrawing socially and emotionally may be a temporary necessity for some people. Do text from time to time to say you are thinking of them.

- Be welcoming to donor conceived children. They will do well in open and loving families of all types.

- Continue to be supportive of the family as children grow and their needs change.

Don't

- Try to 'fix' the problem by making suggestions or giving advice, no matter how well meaning.

- Make assumptions. Ask instead.

- Ask questions beyond those that show that you care. If they are to satisfy your own curiosity, best to keep them to yourself.

- Make remarks that either judge or imply judgement of decisions made.

- Try inappropriate humour about fertility issues to lighten the situation: be guided by your relative or friend.

- Share information about donor conception with others, inside or outside the family, without checking with your relative or friend first.

- Let the fact of donor conception get in the way of loving a child.

Infertility and donor conception: the facts, the practicalities and the law

About one in six heterosexual couples have trouble in conceiving a child. The difficulties are pretty evenly balanced between men and women. Most will eventually conceive with the couple's own eggs and sperm (called gametes) with or without the help of assisted conception procedures such as in-vitro fertilisation (IVF). There are no figures about how many people decide to use donor gametes or embryos, but around 1,500 children are born each year in the UK following donor-assisted treatments at UK clinics licensed by the Human Fertilisation and Embryology Authority (HFEA). A completely unknown additional number are born following donor gamete treatments abroad or as a result of private sperm donation in the UK.

Who uses donor gametes?

Heterosexual couples where one partner (occasionally both partners) is unable to contribute to the conception of a baby. Unless infertility has been known about because of premature menopause, vasectomy or a chromosomal condition, this inability is only likely to have been confirmed following extensive, and sometimes very invasive, testing and possibly many cycles of unsuccessful treatment.

Lesbian or gay couples who use gametes from the opposite sex in order to have a family together. Male couples will also need a surrogate mother.

Single women who decide to have a family on their own will use donor sperm and sometimes donor eggs as well.

Lesbian or gay couples and single women may or may not have fertility issues as well as a biological need for gametes from the opposite sex.

Some people use donor gametes to avoid passing on a serious genetic condition. But infertility is the main reason for using donor conception. The causes of complete infertility in either a man or a woman are many, complex and sometimes remain unexplained, even following sophisticated testing. If you would like to understand more about the causes of infertility the HFEA's website www.hfea.gov.uk has good information on medical and genetic conditions and the range of interventions and procedures that can ease or circumvent the problem.

Who are the donors?

Sperm and egg donors in the UK are mostly recruited via the many specialist fertility clinics situated around the country. All these clinics are licensed by the HFEA. Donating at a clinic is something that can never be done casually. Sperm as well as egg donors have to make a major commitment to changes in lifestyle and regular attendance at the clinic. They also have to be mature enough to understand and accept the responsibilities that come with being identifiable to any child they have contributed to bringing into being, once that child is 18 (see section on Law for more about this).

Some egg donors are women who offer to donate their eggs and who undergo drug induced stimulation in order to produce more eggs than usual in a cycle. These eggs are then used to help one or more women who need donated eggs create embryos using sperm from a partner or a donor.

Egg-share donors are women who are in need of in-vitro fertilisation (IVF) treatment, but do not need donor eggs themselves. In return for reduced treatment fees they agree to share half of the eggs they produce (under stimulated conditions) with a woman who needs donor eggs. In both egg-sharing and direct donation the best embryo or embryos are surgically placed in the uterus of the recipient. All egg donors have to be younger than 36 and sperm donors need to be under 40.

All donors have to undergo standard testing for communicable diseases and for major genetically inherited disorders. A full family medical history is also required. See HFEA website for more information on testing.

Donors at UK licensed centres are only allowed to contribute to 10 families. Egg donors rarely help to create more than two or three families because donating eggs is a lengthy, invasive and time consuming procedure.

As a result of a decision taken in 2011 by the HFEA, from April 2012 direct egg donors have been entitled to compensation of £750 per cycle and sperm donors at £35 per donation, with the possibility of expenses on top. Some donors choose not to take this money.

Egg and sperm donors can be recruited privately via family and friends, through the one or two egg donation agencies in the UK or via web sites where donors and recipients can make contact with each other. As egg donation always involves IVF, a high-tech and invasive procedure, all donors have to be introduced to a fertility clinic in order for the process to take place. In the UK, and most places in the world, donors are counselled before taking part in donation procedures.

Sperm donation, being a simpler process, can take place outside of a licensed clinic. See section about the Law for more information.

Treatment abroad

Over recent years many people have gone abroad for donor conception, particularly egg donation. This is historically because of long waiting lists for egg donors in the UK, the cost of fertility treatment in this country and occasionally because recipients prefer an anonymous donor. Some women needing egg donation are choosing to go to the US or South Africa where considerably more information is available about both egg and sperm donors than in the UK or the rest of Europe. South African egg donors are mostly anonymous whilst it is possible to find an identifiable egg donor in the US, although most are anonymous. Some single women, in particular, choose to import donor sperm from the US, not only to have more information, but also in order to be able to trace other families with children created by the same donor via the number given to a donor by the sperm bank. Only sperm from donors willing to be identifiable can be imported into the UK. In the countries in Europe that are popular with British residents all donors of gametes are anonymous and very little information is available about them. Donors in other countries are paid varying amounts of compensation. The highest fees for both egg donors and assisted conception procedures generally are in the US.

See section on the Law for further information about differences between donation in the UK and abroad.

The Law: The Human Fertilisation and Embryology Act

The HFEA is the body that inspects, regulates and licenses all fertility clinics, assisted conception procedures and research on embryos. It came into being in August 1991 as a result of the Human Fertilisation and Embryology Act being passed in 1990. Since that time the HFEA has kept a register of all fertility treatments where donor gametes have been used, the names and details of recipients and donors and the outcomes of those treatments. Parents of donor conceived children have certain rights to access non-identifying information about their donor. Non-identifying information should be available at the time of treatment, although some clinics hold back some details until a pregnancy is established. Once a child is born parents can apply to the HFEA to find out the number of other children who have been born following help from the same donor, their gender and years of birth.

Between August 1991 and March 2005 all donors were anonymous to both parents and the child. Following consultation the law was amended in 2004 and from April 2005 donors have had to agree to be identifiable to children from the age of 18, on the initiative of the young person. Donors recruited via clinics remain anonymous to the parents.

At any point after donating donors can apply to the HFEA to find out the years of birth and gender of children born as a result of their donation.

They cannot have either non-identifying or identifying information about recipients or children.

Men and women who donated gametes between August 1991 and March 2005 can choose to re-register with the HFEA so that they can become identifiable or they may choose not to do so, thereby retaining their anonymity.

The HFE Act protects all parties to donor conception in the following ways:

Heterosexual and lesbian consenting couples and single women are legally the parents of any child conceived in a licensed clinic. In the case of all couples, both partners' names appear on the birth certificate. As the law currently stands the donor's name or existence is not acknowledged at birth registration or on the birth certificate. The General Register Office has guidance about births where a donor is involved and registrars expect solo mothers to enter Father Unknown in the section for father.

An anonymous donor who donated at a licensed clinic cannot take action to gain access to the child at any time and equally recipients cannot seek financial or any other support for a donor conceived child from a donor.

If sperm or eggs are imported into the UK from abroad and treatments take place in an HFEA licensed clinic then UK laws apply to those donors. Their name, last known address and passport number are recorded and children conceived will have the right to apply for identifying information from age 18.

Donation outside of a licensed clinic

If sperm donation takes place outside of a licensed clinic and couples are married or in a civil partnership, then legal parenthood is established for the male partner in a heterosexual couple or non-birth mother in a lesbian partnership. If a couple are unmarried, not in a civil partnership or a woman is single then the donor is the legal father. Whilst many private arrangements can turn out well, there is an increasing incidence of donors taking women to court seeking access to children that they find they have unexpectedly strong feelings about once they are born. All parties to private donation arrangements should seek legal advice and counselling support before going ahead.

As a result of a UK High Court ruling in February 2013 it has been established that a known donor can apply to the court for contact with a child he has contributed to the conception of, if he has had at least some on-going contact with that child. The donor does not have to be a legal parent in order to make this application and the conception could have taken place inside or outside a licensed clinic.

This is a landmark ruling and does not necessarily establish the right of a known donor to have access to a child.

Donation abroad

Egg, sperm and embryo donation procedures taking place outside of the UK are subject to local laws and regulations. The HFEA has no jurisdiction outside of the UK. No information about donors or children who are born following donated gamete or embryo treatments outside of the UK are recorded on the HFEA Register.

Children conceived abroad have different rights to information than those conceived in the UK. Further information about donor conception abroad can be found in the document Home or Overseas on the DC Network website www.dcnetwork.org

Resources

Books

- Ken Daniels, *Building a family with the assistance of donor insemination* (Dunmore Press, Palmerston North, 2004) Available in the UK only from DC Network

- Ellen Sarasohn Glazer and Evelina Weidman Sterling, *Having your baby through egg donation, Second Edition* (Jessica Kingsley, London, June 2013)

- Diane Ehrensaft, *Mommies, daddies, donors, surrogates: answering tough questions and building strong families* (The Guildford Press, New York, London, 2005)

- Susan Newham-Blake, *Making Finn: one couple's unconventional journey to motherhood* (Penguin South Africa 2013)

- Olivia Montuschi, *Telling and Talking booklets, 0-7, 8-11, 12–16, 17+* (Donor Conception Network, 2006, 0-7 updated 2012, 8-11 updated 2013) Printed and pdf copies available from www.dcnetwork.org

- Olivia Montuschi, *Mixed Blessings: Building a family with and without donor help* (Donor Conception Network 2012) pdf copies only available from www.dcnetwork.org

- *Our Story* children's story books for all family types available from DC Network www.dcnetwork.org

Films

- *A Different Story* (Donor Conception Network, 2003) DVD.
Seven children and young people from heterosexual couple families talk about their thoughts and feelings about being conceived with the help of anonymous sperm donors.
Available to buy or borrow from DC Network library,.

- *Telling and Talking about Donor Conception* (Donor Conception Network 2006) DVD.
Parents and children talk about their experiences of telling. Includes solo mums and a lesbian family.
Available to buy or borrow from DC Network library.

Research on sharing information with others

- *Relative Strangers project* conducted by Professor Carol Smart and Dr. Petra Nordqvist at the Morgan Centre, University of Manchester
March 2013
http://www.socialsciences.manchester.ac.uk/morgancentre/research/relative-strangers/

This research project explored how heterosexual and lesbian couples who conceive using donor sperm, eggs or embryos negotiate telling parents and relatives about their decision to use a donor. Wider family is often very important in the context of having a baby, and the project investigated how couples feel about sharing information about the process of donor conception with their own parents, in-laws, extended families and of course their children.

As part of this project heterosexual and lesbian couples, and also grandparents of donor conceived children, were interviewed about their experiences.

- Petra Nordqvist has also written extensively on lesbian parenthood here:
www.socialsciences.manchester.ac.uk/morgancentre/research/relative-strangers/outputs/index.html.

- Nuffield Council on Bio-Ethics
  Report on Donor Conception: Ethical aspects of information sharing
  April 2013
  www.nuffieldcouncilonbioethics/donor-conception

  This report explores the ethical issues that arise around the disclosure of information in connection with donor conceived people.

Organisations and contacts

British Association for Counselling and Psychotherapy
15 St. John's Business Park
Lutterworth
Leicestershire
LE17 4HB
01455 883300
www.bacp.co.uk
bacp@bacp.co.uk

Donor Conception Network
154 Caledonian Road
London
N1 9RD
020 7278 2608
www.dcnetwork.org
enquiries@dcnetwork.org

Human Fertilisation and Embryology Authority
10 Spring Gardens
St James's
London
SW1A 2BU
020 7291 8200
www.hfea.gov.uk
admin@hfea.gov.uk

Natalie Gamble – Solicitor
Natalie Gamble Associates
19 Glasshouse Studios
Fryern Court Road
Burgate
Nr. Salisbury
Wiltshire
SP6 1QX
www.nataliegambleassociates.com
Natalie@nataliegambleassociates.com
0844 357 1602

Useful websites

Donor Sibling Registry (DSR)
https://www.donorsiblingregistry.com/
The largest and most comprehensive site for connecting donor offspring/donors/half-siblings. Started in the US by Wendy Kramer and her sperm donor conceived son Ryan, it has many entries for UK clinics. In addition to the registry there is an excellent section giving access to up to date research and many ways of connecting with and exploring donor conception issues with others.

Choice Moms.org
www.choicemoms.org

Single Mothers by Choice
www.singlemothersbychoice .org

The two websites above are well-respected, long-standing American organisations for single women who are choosing to become solo mothers.

Fertility Friends
UK based: the largest and best used public infertility/fertility forum
www.fertilityfriends.co.uk

American Fertility Association
http://www.theafa.org/about-the-afa/
A counsellor-led not-for-profit organisation providing supportive and educational materials for anyone looking to build a family and experiencing infertility and/or the need for donated gametes. Inclusive of all family types, this organisation has some excellent short leaflets and podcasts on many aspects of family creation by donor conception.